Life Within Life

I0117210

Hollis Dixon

chipmunkapublishing
the mental health publisher

Published by
Chipmunkapublishing
United Kingdom

http://www.chipmunkapublishing.com

ISBN   978-1-84991-978-4

Chipmunkapublishing gratefully acknowledge the support of Arts Council England.

I believe in telepathy, mind control,
paranormal activity,
and life energy which are in all things.

Telepathy is a thing that everyone experiences but most ignore, dismiss or simply do not believe and put it down as coincidence. Some of my experiences have confirmed to me that it is possible to know what someone else is thinking and also communicate; and it's not only from person to person but also with animals.

One of the examples of which I've seen a lot, is when a person is trying to get another's attention; if this is in a crowded room with lots of noise or a place where shouting is not appropriate, the person will stare at the other, hoping they will look at them or in their direction and in lots of cases, it happens. I believe, in the stare, the intentions are transmitted, and the other will read or feel it, and turn.

I have seen it time and time again. A man or a woman likes the look of the opposite sex in a bar or social setting, he or she looks to admire or whatever; more often than not, the other person would look, whatever happens after that is down to the communication in the glance between them. How many times have you been in a park or leisure complex with your child and you notice that they are doing something which concerns you? You look from a distance and they will turn and look back at you, sometimes people say I could feel them looking at me. This is normally in a situation where there is a grievance or upset or unwanted attention from the other and what is transmitted makes the recipient uncomfortable and uneasy due to the content of what is transmitted. This communication is not always verbal. You can look at someone and just know whether they're happy, sad, upset, or even whether they want to talk to you or leave where they are. You may say it is just one reading facial expressions, but what makes you look in the first place?

I have seen on many occasions a couple whether married or Partners where the attention from a stranger is quickly stopped from continuing just by a look from the other jealous or protective partner, and this is even done when eye contact is not being made with either party. Also there are times where I have looked at a woman who I've never met before and have full eye contact; what I mean by full eye contact is when both eyes connect with each other as in left eye with right eye and right eye with left. The feeling of pleasure is experienced by both; normally smiles all round in these cases. You may not even talk to each other but that moment is remembered. What I think is information, desire or thought which was transmitted between both at that moment. There are many more examples of telepathy, with animals I have had one personal experience which started me thinking. I am the first person to be wary of an unleashed dog on the street or park, but on this occasion I had no fear; I was working as a carer with a family in a nearby town. Twice a week I would go to the house, open the back gate and knock on the back door. This time when I opened the gate there was a very large Rottweiler in the garden. As I opened the gate slightly, the dog looked at me; it was what I call full eye contact where there is some sort of connection. This stare lasted about 5 seconds; initially fear was the feeling when I first saw it, and it decreased as the stare went on. The tightening of my stomach stopped and I felt at ease. The dog turned and walked back into the garden. I had no concern about walking in the garden to the back door. I went inside and the owner said even he wouldn't have done that.

Another situation where true it could be coincidence, is when I was at a friend's house, getting some of my writing typed up... she has cats; I believe 4 at the time... she was sitting there using her laptop and 1 of them started to walk over the keyboard. She gently pushed it off and continued; this happened time and time again. Of course she got a little annoyed by this; the last time it happened, she didn't say anything, she stared at the cat which was next to her with its back to her and she pointed at the door of the room. Straight away the cat turned and left the room.

This brings me to another point; emotion and action: in what I have seen and experienced myself, when a person is emotionally charged, they are more receptive to telepathy and are able to pass on the energy in different means. I believe the life energy which is the result of any emotion can be transmitted or transferred to another person. A stare can make the recipient feel the emotion that a person who's looking is feeling. Also information can be passed from person to person in this way and in most cases where I've seen it, is when either one or both are in an emotional state of mind. This teamed up with an action will affect the recipient more as the action enhances the thought. I used to wonder why I got annoyed in queues; first thought was that I was impatient but 1 day I was standing in a queue in a petrol station and I started to get uncomfortable; it so happened that there was a mirror over the till point and I noticed a man behind me staring at the back of my head and rocking, I thought this was strange behaviour; another thing, he was standing close; within my personal space or aura. I find that a person within about a metre or so from you; you can feel. I took a mental note of this and continued to watch out for it. It happened time and time again. The action of the other person may change but the stare or focus on me was the same. And it always made me uncomfortable or annoyed. Many times the person was outside my personal space but the stare and action at the same time had the same effect. Normally in these cases in the first instance the person will talk loudly or grab my attention somehow so there would be eye contact first. In 1 instance in a queue at a bank, the effect on me was so bad it was instant severe depression. That has only happened to me twice; the first time it knocked me out for a good few months, I just couldn't function. I had to move out of the family home, lost my business I was running and my life went to pot, all because of a 15 second situation. In that instance I had eye contact with the person but didn't see the action.

There are other things that I think aid the link from person to person; familiarity; knowing the person or having information about them. Many times, too many to mention, I have known what a partner is going to say next; it could be me knowing their habits or their trends of thoughts, but I think it's more than that, for instance they would ask me maybe to go to the shop and I would think of items on the list before they say them. I was on the phone to my girlfriend; we were deciding where to go out for the day. As we pondered in silence an overwhelming thought came to me in my head and as the thought stopped, she mentioned the place I was thinking about. Obscure details of a conversation which weren't mentioned at the time come to light as time goes on within day to day chats between the two of us.

Another thing I believe in is collective thought; this is when a number of people have the same similar thought and are able to change the thoughts of others or a lesser amount of people and this is the result of the power of life energy of the majority. You can put this in context of reading the daily papers; millions read them and as a result have the same or similar thoughts on the issues outlined. Those who have a different view due to thinking outside the box or reading between the lines are influenced not only by the conversations of the contents of the papers, but the thoughts which are transmitted from person to person in every day contact they have with one another. This as I see it is a way of keeping the masses on the same page, therefore a type of control to keep things within a predictable and controllable state.

Mind control is a thing which happens every day in normal situations which everybody accepts. Disciplining a child, you make them know that if they don't behave there will be consequences, therefore by giving them a choice which is pleasant and a choice which is not, hoping that they choose the pleasant one which is what you want them to do. Then there is the word dropping where words are dropped into conversations causing the listener to subconsciously take them on board and use them to come to any given conclusion or action which they think is their own, but it isn't because the information given to make the decision was craftily given to them and the decision is what the giver is wanting as a result. What I mean is if you say a certain word that subconsciously directs the thought process to images and meanings of the said word. If I said ghost, then images of a transparent or dream like person would come to mind, provoking feelings of fear and thoughts of dead people; images of horror films may come to mind. A person knowing this mind process could construct and guide a conversation which has only 1 resulting thought, therefore controlling your action. Also, when words are said, accompanied with a gesture or action at the same time, subconsciously has more substance and affects the recipients subconscious more. A pointed finger or another hand gesture, even a nod of the head can emphasise the word. This is all taken in to the subconscious of the listener and I believe that by using telepathy as the voice aspect of the situation accompanied with an action which is seen or not seen by the recipient, still can have the same outcome.

Mind control which causes certain actions and decisions by a recipient doesn't have to be caused by their own thoughts or intentions but by another. Just as I could know what my girlfriend was going to say before she said it on the phone, over a great distance; as long as there is some sort of contact beforehand, or information of each other known, thoughts can be transmitted and received. This does depend on the matter of emotional energy in the sender and that is any emotion, if what I think on this point is right then I would say that some of the thoughts that people have in everyday life are not their own and they don't even realise. Thoughts that make decisions, thoughts that are acted upon with the outcome not what the recipient wants or to the benefit of the recipient but of the sender. The stronger mind will overcome the weaker. Stronger as in belief in what the person thinks, their confidence, factual knowledge and faith, and weaker as in confused, unsure, low self-esteem and confidence. A conversation is had with the aim to put a person in a state of so-called weaker minded state, even when the stronger minded person can succumb to the effects of either word or telepathic mind control.

One of the common factors is life energy; this energy is a build-up of emotion within oneself which can be channelled into whatever task you want, if you know how. It can create a mind state which allows you to transmit and receive thoughts through telepathy. It can give you strength of mind if it is used right. It can change your perception of life by showing you things which one ignores, dismisses or just not believed due to the normal mind state of people. It can give you the ability to control others, although this sounds like a good thing, as we know man is selfish and the capabilities of life energy can be and are used for personal gain. Rationally thinking, I believe it is down to the knowledge and understanding of a person; say for instance that a person saw something out of the ordinary like an image walking through an unopened door, picking up a cup and walking out with it; in his mind whether it was an illusion or fact, he saw it and it will be believed because it was his or her experience. Now this person and another are in a situation where a set of keys are missing, they went missing at night and in the morning all doors were locked and there was no signs of a break-in; the person who had the strange experience would be better equipped to remain stable in this situation as his own understanding and knowledge would be able to come to a rational conclusion. The person without the strange experience would not be able to come to a satisfying conclusion because his own experiences do not give him the answer to the situation. This is knowing that neither of them hid or lost the keys in the first place. An extreme example I know, but factual knowledge is priceless, not hearsay, gossip or fiction. What you know is what you have experienced. All the rest is speculation. It can be considered, but not truly believed or taken as facts. So when it comes to the stronger mind; believing in your own experience is needed no matter how strange. So in everyday life, the one who saw the image go through the wall will be seen as the unstable one and made to think that him or herself, but in fact the second person is the one who is unstable in this situation because he has no logical conclusion to come to; therefore will be unsure, less confident in him or herself.

Logical progress is thinking things which are not the norm, but people who do this are thought of as ill in some way or another. The perception of life gained by thinking like myself; a diagnosed schizophrenic answers many questions which people just push aside or just remain sceptics on the issue. They say that we don't know the answer, but it's not that. That attitude is normally because it doesn't fit in with moral, religious law or the general function of society.

Money goes where money is to be made. With access to money your ability to make things happen in your life and others increase the more money you have, the more you have, the more chances of having a lifestyle you like and peace of mind, and also allows you to live how you want and by your rules. Money is a thing which most people think is a means to progress through life. The more you have, the easier and more pleasant the life experience. This attitude in my eyes is giving permission to the powers that be to control, dictate and abuse. The fact that you are taught from an early age that life is supposed to have certain elements in it; like a good education, good job, be married with kids, your own home etc. the pressure to achieve these things are immense but we don't realise it and this is just the beginning. The influence of music, sport, advertising, the rich and famous and there are many more, all add to the pressure to achieve so one can reach the level of lifestyle which is seen to be acceptable. The judge of what is acceptable is not only society but children, parents, grandparents, peers, partners and the list goes on, and they all have different opinions. Then there is work, a place where your efforts can make all the pressure go away if your wage allows you to satisfy all the expectations of others; but this in itself is more pressure as you have to please others to earn the wage that allows you to have a peaceful and stress free life. Therefore putting the people who judge your efforts in a position of power over you, which I see knowing how human nature is like putting your head in a noose. Also this type of pressure can put one in an emotional and weaker mind state that can be easily manipulated.

As we all know, many people will do all sorts of things to get ahead. The colleague at work that steals your idea, the country that uses its influence, its power and its resources to gain control over another. It has been shown in history that people will go to serious lengths to achieve their goal and if that means stepping on the less fortunate man, it is done.

I wrote about paranormal activity in my first book: "Life". My experiences were things like seeing a figure enter a room through an unopened door. A glass on a draining board turned over a number of times without any physical contact.

Voices heard in other rooms of my flat when there were no persons present. Figures, like dark shadows with their body language and gestures seeming to communicate with me. Feelings of someone or something touching me with no physical presence seen, a movement on my bed; like someone getting on it and lying next to me. A presence felt and with that, the process and rationalisation of thought was beyond my comprehension. I've also seen a large cloud which was moving in the opposite direction to the others and causing a large shadow as it moved over the landscape without any sight of the sun. A feeling of being guided around the streets by a force which is physical and pushes you in one direction or another. All these in the daytime as well as the night, within or outside buildings. All these experiences were had without any mind altering substances. I believe that what most say is paranormal is just a part of nature, which like the depths of the sea, man hasn't seen or can't explain. All of these influences, seen and unseen that people experience, sometimes aware and sometimes not, shape our lives, personalities and situations we go through. With knowledge of these elements and how they work, whether people on mass or individually can be controlled to a point; someone once said "life is what happens to you while you're busy making other plans". A simple wedding engagement which most see as a journey, a church service and a reception, is much more. Everything you see and hear on the journey there; the interaction, seen and unseen at the church, the vibe and the aura of each person there, the careless attitudes of the guests at the reception, the collective thought of all the people at the event. All these and more affect and influence all involved, also the paranormal or nature aspects which I have explained will affect, influence and guide each person without them knowing it.

With all that I have said, is man controlling man with all the ways of communication? Or is it nature controlling man to do so, like the animals of the world; what tells the grazer to move pasture to pasture and what direction to move? What tells the eagle how to find his mate, miles from where they are? Who tells the insect where to make its home where his food is plentiful? Is it just nature? This is just my opinion and after all; I'm just a paranoid schizophrenic.

Hollis Dixon

Just My Opinion

Hollis Dixon

It takes all sorts to make a world

The Dr who knows enough about the body to heal. The homeless person who knows how to keep warm on a winter's night and can advise those in same situation. The person who tends the land to produce elements of a roast we have on Sunday afternoon. The addict who knows the pit falls of substance abuse. The person who has had so many traumas in their lives and got through it. That could be a counsellor without training. The disabled person who's heightened senses has made them an expert in care of the restricted. The person with a disorder who brings joy to others with their creative talents. Or the blind person who's view of the world inspires others.

It takes all sorts to make a world.

All they do

Your aim is to build on life
But you do much more
Instilling confidence, self-worth and reason for life
Making light of the problem, turmoil's and strife's
I owe you more than you know
In life I will make best
As you have taught me so

It's just is

Wrong or right or is it pleasant or unpleasant. The law and morals of most are governed by the government, religion and what we find pleasing or unpleasing to the individual amongst other things. A situation to one person is normally gauged on if it is beneficial or pleasant to that individual and given the labels, good or bad or wrong or right. If a situation is unpleasant for one person, stopping them from reaching their goals and aims, and the same situation is pleasant or right for another at the same time. This makes me think that the labels that will be given to these events or happenings don't exist. Therefore there is no wrong or right there is just is. The feelings and emotions we feel are just our reactions to the mental understanding of the situation. And I will add that it is only the individual's aims which determine the labels.

I Remember

Remember when I was young
The party at my brothers was all well and done
It was a young lady that caught my eye
Thin, dark eyes and lovely within
The time came at the end of the night
Where all in the house had to turn in
We went together, the same door we went in
As I was young and love was a stranger
But by sunrise I knew it well.

Contradiction

Thinking about what I have been through, good and bad. Its seems that some, not all, find it fascinating and have a large interest in the types of things which have happened or is happening in the strange and paranormal life which has chosen me. This brings me to the question, why do the professionals aim to dampen or even eliminate the very thing which brings them to work every morning. I am not saying all but some enjoy and see that the weird and wonderful things that a client or service user says and explains, is of a greater interest really than the aim to guide and condition them to be integrated back into the normal way of thinking and society. And as the continuous line of clients open up to them on a daily basis year after year. Some re-joining the normal way of life, which I see it is not them and some continue to feed the thrust of the professionals. Have they thought that if it is fascinating to them, then to the person who is living it, is fascinated by it to but has a ring side seat of something that should be embraced and seen as a gift and not dampened and suppressed. The dilemma of being told you must change the way you think is not good to hear. Just because society says that it is so, doesn't mean that its right and everyone has to think by the same rules.

How life is

I see life as a series of actions, reactions, words and most importantly thoughts and life energy. Life energy can be transmitted and received from person to person whether positive or negative or as I would rather say pleasant or unpleasant. Words cause the build-up of energy given what we understand them to mean and how they affect the individual. The actions and reactions also cause build-up of energy but this happens more subconsciously as to consciously read a person's body language, is something which is alien to most. But a movement, a gesture, an expression is read by the subconscious mind. The thought and intention of a person can be felt and reacted upon without one even being aware. If you put this all together you get a complex network of communication between people which we are sometimes aware of and sometimes not. The communication will affect all of our emotions also causing us to act in a certain manner. A person walking past your house with the correct combination of life – energy, thought and intention will attract you to look out the window at them or in their direction or repel you to do the opposite. If the energy is strong enough, the person could be in the next street, or even further. This would prompt you to go for a walk or pop to the shop, so seeing them or connecting with them in some way is, in some way completed and if they were repelling you then a pop to the shop would be unpleasant and even if you walked by them there would be no interaction between you both, so bearing this in mind, everything that happens is down to the life force between every one of us. Nothing is not supposed to happen, like an unplanned meeting, a smile from a stranger, or you turning up somewhere and being needed or seeing something you should or shouldn't have. There are no coincidences, but I see that the structure and aim of society hampers this process and the natural flow is distorted, causing unpleasant things to happen i.e.; wars, riots, upheavals... all because the incentive of life is not part of the natural force that we are all governed by. If we all did what we felt to do, pushing aside that we would be up too late or not spending enough time at home or taking an extra 10 minutes at lunchtime at work; true the normal structure of life will be damaged not to say the economy, but surely man trying to create and control something as powerful as natures force is suicide.

The Council

When I was homeless living in my car outside a disused builders compound. I used to experience a thing I call the council. About 2 months into the homeless situation, at night sometime late in the evening as I sat in the driver's seat, looking into the night sky and over the waste land in front, I would hear voices talking in firm tones. They would sound like they were coming from all different directions and not as thoughts or voices in my head which I have experienced before. These voices would talk about everything and anything. The feeling was not that they were talking to me, but just voicing their opinion. There would be so many of them that it would be like I was in a large hall filled with people, all talking at the same time. As time went on I made my conclusion that these were the subconscious thoughts of people and their true opinion of life and the world. I listened night after night, from late evening to about midnight or soon after. I was tempted to join in by shouting but somehow I knew that that was not the way it was done. As I listened, the thought came to me that even though I couldn't hear what each individual was saying, somehow in my mind the information of each person was still being logged and remembered in my mind.

This went on for about two weeks. The last night it happened the voices as usual talked over each other until a strong thought and feeling came to me, in my mind. It said what's your opinion?, I paused for a moment then I just focused on one area of the sky and let my mind go blank, and with that, it was like a dictated passage of words flew through my mind. The voices got quieter and quieter as my focused stare projected into the sky. There was a feeling of calm and clarity in the air, contentment and reassurance. The voice stopped and I have not heard the council since.

Tree Seasons

As I look out of my window at a tree top which towers over the houses beneath, a series of branches and twigs, which only a lover of nature would see as beautiful. Strong and elegant in its stance, enduring the bitter cold breeze of the winter months. The view changes slightly. The branches and twigs start to grow green, and the next generation of fruit. The plain silhouette changes its form as life begins again. Life which is all but genius as its life sustains ours. The leaves and blossom have done their part. As seen by most as beauty. The silhouette is full and lush hiding many other living things within. All that have benefited are now on their own journey to a warmer place. The cold bitter winds return, the lush green canopy turns into a ray of colours that decorate the floor around its trunk. Giving way to the plain silhouette of branches and twigs I first saw. Strong and elegant in its stance.

Homeless

Homeless for three and half months. Living in my car in front of a compound of wild flowers and weeds. This time was a mixed bag of emotion and events. The first night I was relieved to be out of the situation I left behind. Its stress free with a feeling of independence. Uncomfortable to sleep but at least was out of the wind and rain. As time went on other things came to light, like the solitude the lack of communication to others, the feeling of being banished from society for some reason. Only my thoughts would comfort me when I was hungry and had no money or cold in the early morning before the sun came up. The thought of people saying and thinking things about me. People started to shy away from me, as word got out that I was the one living in his car in that layby. I kept as clean as I could by using water and baby wipes, but still looks were like I was covered in mud. Money was short, sometimes a packet of custard creams or packet of crisps was my only meal for the day.

But I enjoyed that I was close to nature. Watching the family of pheasants grow from chicks to their first day of flight. Watching the falcon hunt over the wasteland in front of me. Being woken up by the family of crows in the early morning with their loud squawks. Hares playing and boxing behind the compound gates. The foxes that prowl around in the evening causing the male pheasant to let out its warning cries. This gave me hope and strength; I guess I turned to the one thing that didn't judge me.

Time

I have noticed that most people are obsessed with time. People, business, government. From the everyday people to the scientists and the inventors that shape our world.

My thoughts on time are that it is just a mathematical way to add structure to an already structured world. The only difference is that most of the structure put in place is to make money. The time we get up in the morning and have meals. Have time to ourselves or with our family or friends, is basically dictated to us. The control of each person is governed by work school and law. Time is just a means of structuring people. Take the night; the main reason for people sleeping at night is so they are not tired at work. The night should be experienced not only to party and paint the town red. Try going for a walk at 3 in the morning, the quiet, peaceful bliss that it is. The vibe is different and nice. I found you can think clearer at night, the atmosphere is cleaner, more pleasant. I believe it's a very special time which most miss out on due to the structure of time.

MY FATHER

He taught me right and wrong, by his example
He taught me consideration and love, by his example
He taught me to be humble, by his example
And showed me a level of consciousness
towards life and his surroundings
that I only can strive to achieve.
My father taught me

Dreaming

As I lay my head down to rest, and the day's events I digest
A dream of me amongst the trees of a beautiful forest I see,
I run and jump with a bouncing motion.
With each leap I increase my height
Till I do not return to the ground,
I soar and take flight
The lush green canopy I see of the forest and the meadows
below.
The feeling is so free and effortless.
Happiness at its best, no sorrow, no doubt
As all things, it does come to an end.
When I swoop down too low to the ground
And my feet make contact
there the sensation stops, and I lay and rest.

FREEDOM

Some say freedom is a word for nothing left to lose.
I say freedom is knowing what is important.
You may have everything in the world, but know what is not worth
worrying about, losing gives you freedom of mind spirit and body.
Therefore you don't have to lose them to know

EMOTIONS

Emotions are there to be to be had. They are meant to happen in any given situation. Whether they are pleasant or unpleasant you should embrace them, learn from them. Ask yourself why I felt that, was it a word, an action, a thought that caused it. Was it I who instigated the process of actions and reactions that built up to the feeling? Was it within your power to control the events or feelings? Or was it a thing which no man or woman can ever control.
I think that the first step to emotional success is to accept that you are not perfect, and in turn understand that others are not perfect too.

Destiny

What you see you are supposed to see,
What you hear you are supposed to hear,
All your experiences are yours alone,
Try and avoid them,
You will think them anyway.
Your reaction to them is down to you.

Wealth

I notice from talking to different people that when I explain that I have been through hardships such as homelessness, substance abuse and family break ups. An example of a celebrity or person they know has come through a trying time, and now is wealthy and successful within the social setting of the world. I believe that he has not become wealthy at all, but is selling the wealth that he had gained when he or she was, as we see it going through rough times. Now he is just trading it in for material wealth.

What I see

Sitting looking from my second floor flat, watching as the raging wind battering the trees in the view of the green belt land between me and next village. The wind tosses the branches to and fro, testing the strength and capabilities of the trees ability to withstand the rough and harsh treatment of nature. But the tree is part of nature too. And it evolves to withstand this treatment and grows ever stronger as time goes on.

What I draw from this what I see, is the sometimes harsh treatment that a person can experience from life, is not a negative and should be seen as opportunity to grow strong and prepare themselves for things that possibly may lay ahead.

To you am grateful

My experiences and the treatment I have received by others
has made me what I am. And within my understanding of
what can be done in life. I will walk tall and live.
To all I am grateful.

The Flag

I suggest we have a human flag. A Flag that represents all that is good about humans, as we have flags for each country of the world. You may say this is pointless, as whom would we show it to. Who would see it and realise that humans are different from them.

So why do we do this within the world, with countries having individual flags. This is pointing out that there are differences between us, which breeds thought of I'm better than you. And with that why are we seen as different in the first place. A human is a human. The influences and what we are taught makes us different.

The Munchkin

At first you may say why
And he may ask himself too
The driven attitude he has
To get through to you
He may ruffle a few feathers
But he makes people smile
Some points you may cringe
Like you're watching a child
A thought becomes an idea
The idea an action
And before all around knows
It's the next big attraction
A big part he plays
As he moves from group to group
Like he is spinning a web of wellbeing
So all can survive

Silent World

Solitude, silence, is that a personal want or a reaction. Not without the lack of trying to communicate and take part in the social pastime of community. But find yourself met with the preconceptions and judgement by many. Which dismisses your voice and words before you say them. Attitudes that with ignorant understanding and knowledge crush the very being of a person. This forcing one to relay on the small and simple actions to make or break their day. A smile from a stranger, and door being opened. A phone call which shows that you have not been forgotten. Someone moves closer and not away shows that your vibe is not repelling. These all from those who have no way of knowing you have been labelled with a diagnosed heading from those you give a name to something which they don't understand. To some from professional to man on the street, when you have been given that label your personality is dead, and you become a textbook case with no rational voice. Identity removed, your life continues. Relying on what it says in the books that explains the personality you have. No longer knowing whether you are right or wrong in your thoughts, you plod alone in the system from that day on.

Love Is

Love is as I see it, when a person takes into consideration all
that is pleasant and unpleasant with another person, and
accepting it without judgement. And will do their utmost to
ensure that the person's happiness, wellbeing and
contentment are achieved. Also enjoy doing so.
My question is can it truly be achieved knowing the
personalities, attitudes and personal aims of a human being.

Someone said to me

It's not that I want to but it's that I like to know I have the choice.

This at the time made me think an array of things. That the person was just being selfish and wanted their own way, without thinking or taking into consideration other people. That this person didn't care about the effects of their actions when it came to other people. That this person was planning to do something which would not be good for me. Therefore asking me for permission without asking me a straight forward question. It took me a while to really come to terms with this, even though I agreed at the time. But now I realise what this person was saying.

Life has many restrictions. Your job has rules and policies. The way you conduct yourself in society is restricted by the laws of the land. Your behaviour is governed by your parents, teachers and elders. Your freedom of thought is governed by morals and principles of what you have been taught. The list goes on. This I see is very mentally frustrating to say the least, when a person is trying to achieve a goal.

All this person was saying to me was let me be free in your eyes. I see now that freedom of mind is important for personal growth. This I see, when I'm looking around, is lacking. Also that the frustrations which are caused by these rules, policies and laws are not helping with the emotional stability of many.

Sad but true

Just like a farmer can see from when a seedling is young
Whether it will be a good crop or not and act accordingly.
So can a person can see whether another will be beneficial
to them
And do the same.

Thoughts

We have evolved naturally to do unnatural things.

Curiosity was the beginning and it shall be the end.

Don't focus on the problem, focus on the solution.

Man makes law of the world, but nature's law has the answers.

Believe everything but act on nothing until you know.

We are all part of a man made evolution.

If you find that you need something to live. Learn to live without it.

Happiness is but a moment, but contentment can last forever.

In all that you do there is a purpose.

Thoughts

An opinion is just that, an opinion.

What I don't understand I try to accept.

To find reason you must have knowledge.
Only using your own knowledge you will find acceptance,
As to truly understand another is impossible.

I belong and feel at home in a natural spiritual world. My life
is but a stepping stone to reach that existence.

Many would rather you think that you are ill, than for you to
know the truth.

At times it's not for you to understand but for you to accept.

Don't let your kindness be seen as weakness.
What you crave is what you need.

Thoughts

Things don't get better or worse, things that change are just different.

The first step to emotional success is accepting that you are not perfect

Admitting that you are wrong is not a moment of weakness but a moment of strength as you have the ability to face truth.

Anger is a product of misunderstanding.

If you can think it, you can achieve it. Identify each obstacle and overcome them one by one.

If man only uses what nature has given him, how far up the food chain would we be.

Until a human can prove to me that he or she has the gift of ultimate knowledge. I will not let anything said make me doubt myself.

Thoughts

There is no such thing as time. The sun rises and it sets
then there is night. There are seasons and who knows there
might be another cycle of some sort. Time is just a
manmade mathematical structure which governs our lives.
Rational thinking is only as good as the individual's
knowledge and understanding.

A perfectionist is a person who achieves something to the
best of their ability with the resources they have.

If a person is capable of asking a question, then they are
capable of handling the truthful answer.

Personal success will come because money is not the issue,
aim or incentive.

When some faith is shown to you. Then faith will grow within
Every morning the master plan of life starts. My first breath is
accompanied with the thought, I am part of it and I am as
important as anyone else.

Thoughts

It's not what you believe in, it's the fact you believe.
The truth is within you, know yourself
Validate, Rationalise, Accept and move on.
You can't control anybody but yourself be responsible for your action.
Freedom of mind is knowing what is important.
The understanding of yourself, will help you understand others.
The fight is within, not with others, the key is to accept.
It only takes a moment to change your life.
Another day another opportunity
Use your good days to make sure that the bad days don't happen.
When did we stop doing what is good for us and doing only what's expected.
Believe in yourself and anything is possible
You without influence is yourself, learn to just be.
It's not for them to accept you it's for you to accept yourself.

Last Words

If I have hurt, upset or caused any discomfort in your life
I am sorry
If I have helped, encouraged or made your life better.
It was my pleasure
Just because you can't see me, doesn't mean that I am not
there.
You can feel me and think me.
If you need help or my advice, I have already told you.
You just have to remember.
Live and love life.

I explain and express all my
Experiences within the boundaries of the English langue.
But I do say one doesn't really know unless you
Experience it yourself.

No Labels No Limitation

Untitled Works
By Travis

Hollis Dixon

Biography

Born in 1966 in Royston, Hertfordshire I was given the name Travis. I was raised with my brother who is 9 years older than me. My parents divorced when I was 7. My brother and I were raised by my mother, we saw our father periodically.

I completed my education starting in remedial classes. I completed my education. Work life started at 16, a live in job as a kennel hand. I have had a wide variety of jobs all ending due to illness.

I have been married and divorced twice. During my second marriage I / we had 3 daughters. The relationship ended in divorce in 1998, leaving me to raise my children alone.

I'd had many breakdowns in my teens, early twenties but no intervention from social services. I approached G.P for counselling, he advised against it, I insisted. Turned out G.P was right. In 2000 I was admitted into psychiatric hospital for a short stay. Just 6 weeks later I was re – admitted and put under a section. I was33, a single parent, very frightened and psychotic medication was introduced, monitored, a care plan was put in place, weekly support, many labels later in 2005 I was finally given the diagnosis of schitz affective disorder. My spiritual beliefs were discouraged repeatedly told I had a mental health condition... I'm still in two minds about this. I have a dislike of labels. My experiences include audio, visual disturbances. I became manic then very low.

Once I had started to accept my condition I engaged with art and writing poems, short stories, my turnaround began.

I have had poems published, artwork displayed. I facilitate art and craft workshops for other service users. I also facilitate a hearing voices group.

No longer drowning in unexpressed emotions as writing is my release and my art an expression of me, self-styled, self-taught. Spiritually guided, I'm inspired by nature, driven by the torments in my mind. Armed with insight, awareness I'm still working towards overcoming self-doubt, battling with my condition, stigma of mental illness. I became a volunteer for mind also involved with other mental health organisations.

As the tension builds
The doodles begin
Helps the healing
The release of the din
A distraction from what goes on within

A must
Full of meaning
Allow the emotions to flow
Go where they want to go
Safe within a comfort zone

To off load creatively
Has always been
A personal key to aid my recovery

My creations allow me to breathe
Which enables me to engage
With my being
Just to be
Quiet and still
Within my shell
Time out from a living hell

Travis

With faceless expression
Deep blank stares
Living in and out of daily expression
Countless tears
In a state of regression
The training of the already trained
By the professionals of the mentally strained
On-going recovery from a personal hell
From deep within the secrets hidden
As silence breaks
Tales being told, experience unfolds
What lessons does each of us hold?
(from breakdown to breakthrough)

Travis

What is going on
The lost plot revisited
When the drugs
Have no effect
Lost plot revisited
Psychosis
Is there any way back
Time and time again
Will this living hell
Ever end. I'll never be the same

Travis

Hollis Dixon

Who's playing me?
Who am I
Who could I be
Who am me?
All alone
Trapped in a dome
Lifeless
But not free

Travis

Leaving havoc in its wake
A harrowing, tormented state
Break the shackles
Run from the hate
Seek help before it's too late

Travis

A notepad and pen
Are my only friends
Unconditional
Always around
Tools to offload
What's written from manic mind?
As I unwind
A cuppa, a fag
But best of all
My friend in hand

Travis

Milestones
Moving on
Pushing forward
Being strong

Being strong
Moving forward
Milestones overcome

Travis

Keep it simple
Keep it small
Keep it realistic
Or not at all

Travis

Light illuminates my path with energy
Energy that I haven't had in years
Torment, grief pulling me down
Advice taken from those who have
Travelled in darkness before me
Also from those who have walked towards a new dawn

No more fragmented prison
But a strong diamond
Ready to cut through the old
And set in the new

Balanced and polished
Helped by others
To shine through the darkness

Allowing the past to guide you on
Move forward feeling strong

Travis

Pull up a chair
Find a seat
Gather yourself
Say hello, meet and greet
Body language, eye contact too
Reframing our life skills
That's why we are here
Retracing the battle fields
The painful experiences of our pasts
A mentor or peer, to guide at last
Someone who has been there too
May I (we) learn from you
To help others believe
Help to recognise within yourself
How to overcome the chains of negativity
The qualities that each of us hold
Our true potential, encouraged
Allow new growth to unfold
Finding new direction, goals
On a journey of personal growth
Self-styled healing, self help
My reality was over ridden
I'm breaking free
Out of a self-made prison

Travis

Sit and listen the ideas that unravel
The questions provoke even more mind travel
Work through the map in our minds

An idea, a thought
How to turn it into reality
From out of the matter
Into something solid and true

Share a piece of the dream
With the tools of experience
Work as a team
A brighter future
Lies in store
If you choose to walk through the door

Travis

Working towards a goal or two,
Work alongside me!
May I work with you?
Now let the anchoring begin
Kick off your shoes
Feel the ground beneath your feet
Close your eyes
Listen to your heart beat
Calm the activity in your mind
Once your mind is empty
A blank canvas
Becomes our / your given space,
Embrace
Work together at a steady pace, no need to fear
What brought you here?
Take time, no need for haste.
Silence shared
Then the past retraced
The bringing together
The here and now
Focus on the chosen goal
Retraining the past
Burned away, never seen layers upon layers of deposited
grief.
This offloading, a positive relief

Travis

Surrounded by a man made shell
A crust formed
To protect, somehow

As the cracks start to appear
The pain oozes out
I fear – I'm full of doubt
With no idea
No clue what it's all about

The fear trapped beneath my skin
Provoked by torment of my past
Drowning in unexpressed hopelessness
How to release it
Became my quest

Travis

A well-being meaning
I recognise my feelings
And where I'd like to be

To be able to recognise within myself
What I'm able to see in others
Can those qualities
Really shine through

Insight, awareness
Are these the key?
Highlight my strengths
Work on areas of weakness too

Then another door opens
This time I'm free
From what was holding me back
And messing with my reality

As I'm guided through
New direction
Away from misery
A turn around
Full of possibility
My past is part of me but not all of me

Travis

To all misfits and rebels alike
The highly opinionated
Take a hike
I'm an individual
Who feels the need to write
Contribute something
For others to read even if its shite

Travis

Tit 4 tat
Got to watch out
4 that
Had enough
Of being taken for a prat

It was hard to hear
The words you spoke my dear
Some were harsh, tough
But they were received
Loud and clear

Amidst adversity
Something good will prevail
Over all the pain
Form this living hell

Travis

The evening rush is about to start
I must admit
Straight from the heart
I'm going to bed
It must be said
I can't deal with the mess, extra pressures
And my manic head
I feel the need to hide away
As I've nothing
To smile about today

Travis

Finding it hard
To keep the positives strong
With a struggle
I'll battle on
Trying to keep life simple
Trying to keep life simple
Trying not to see it
As one big con

Travis

Fragments of a shattered mind
Self-expression
Creative schemes
Rainbow reflections
Crazy to some, it must seem

Mystic rainbow waters gleam
A crystal gem
To help heal and restore
The memories we / I have to learn to adore

Travis

Colours adorn the forest floor
Fallen leaves adrift
A carpet of colour
That blankets the ground
Ripe berries on the bushes
Branches hanging heavy with the fruit
The evergreens lush in vibrant colour
The first frosts starch the foliage
Which crunches underfoot
Moisture in the air
Forms water droplets on the grass
Wet pavements display different tones
Within the stone at last
Mini streams form and flow
Temperatures plummet to zero
Dark evenings draw in
Cosy up beside an open fire
Warm at last from head to toe
Soak up the warmth
Enjoy the glow
The trees all bare
The landscapes as one
A single colour

Travis

The snow falls
Chills the air, snuggle indoors without a care

Travis

Mind and matter
I don't mind
But it all matters
In two minds
My mind's eye is shut

I can't hear what I see
I can't see what I hear

Am I here
Who am I
Lost it
Falling apart

A shattered time
With voices fed
No rest inside my head
Armed with matter
The voices charge
A manic mind

I live with this
Most of the time
But still it doesn't matter
For I am just another nutter

Travis

Here I sit
And wonder why
Why the hell
I can't die

Three very special reasons
To stop the above

The voices taunt me
Others will never really know

The pain of my past
Cripples me so

Travis

Its guidance I seek
Due to feeling a freak
Lack of understanding
Judgements, criticism

I find it, maddening
All the pressure from never being clear

Confusion, whilst being misled
All because of my bloody head
All I ever hear, all that's ever said

Have you been messing with your med's

Travis

Here I sit (again)
Scared to live
Yet sparing others from grief

I ponder over the times
I've longed to die

Now faced with a???????
From which I can't hide

The choice is mine
Got to survive
Or be it a natural suicide

Self-neglect, a nasty twist
I've come through psychosis
Just to face this

The curse from childhood past
Another of life's hard knocks
I'm tired of all the bollocks

Travis

So ashamed, ashamed of me
I'm so ashamed of my life's journey
Ashamed of my life cant anyone see
I do have pride, oh let me be

A disappointment that's all I've been
That's all I've achieved
This my legacy

I need to make changes
Need to start again
Replace the misery, it has to end

I must do it now, make a start
Must do better to mend my heart
Build a happy home
One of which I can be proud

It's down to me to change
What took no time to get in a state?
Will take a lifetime
To clear all the hate
This is not how it was meant to be
Now's the time to replace the painful memories
Then I'll be free of being
Ashamed of me

Travis

]A different head
The sixth today
Not one more or any less
I hear them say
This is the crap
That rattles about my head
Slightly numbed by all the med's

To offload the stuff that's there
With or without any care
Its driving me crazy and into despair

Travis

In a place of self-doubt
A shadow surrounds me
Look out of the window
What can I see – life

The life that's troubling me
A daily fight, but today I'm weak
Cancel it all, I've had a terrible week
Not reliable, but continue to try

Guts feel empty. knotted
Legs like jelly, hands all clammy
Trembling inside
Bad thoughts racing in my head
All this time I must hide

I just need to be still
Re-charge my mind
Take a pill
To calm the anguish
And silence the voices
Don't need to reach for the booze

No need to be pissed
Regain control
I will get through this

Travis